I0817164

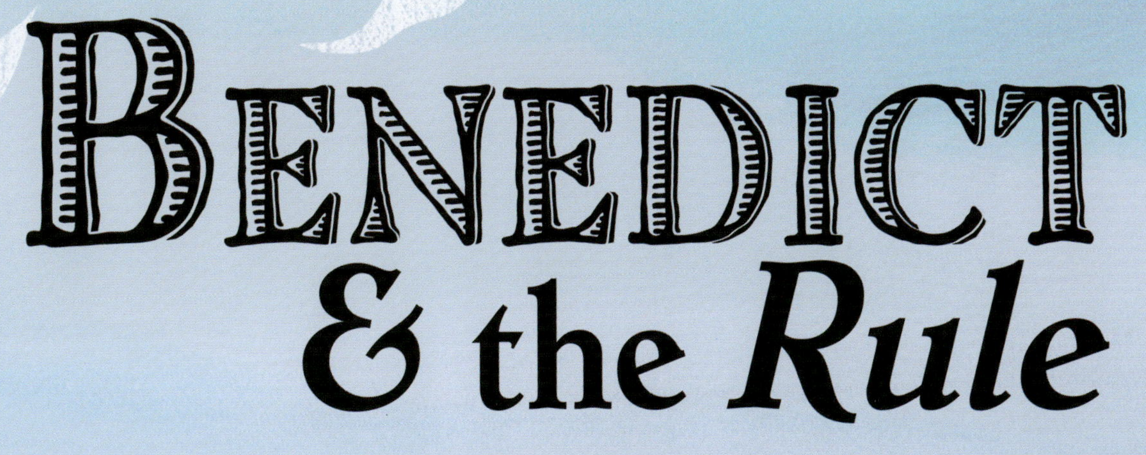

BENEDICT & the *Rule*

written by Katie Warner
illustrated by Leah Ballard

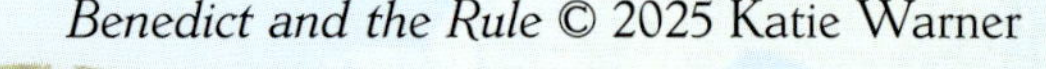

Cover and interior illustrations by Leah Ballard
Typesetting by Meg Whalen

ISBN: 978-1-5051-3527-5
Kindle ISBN: 978-1-5051-3714-9
ePUB ISBN: 978-1-5051-3713-2

Published in the United States by
TAN Books
PO Box 269
Gastonia, NC 28053

www.TANBooks.com

Printed in India

In loving memory of Josh Jarrell,
faithful soldier of Christ, and for his
inspiring family.

K.W.

For my husband, and our
first born daughter.

L.B.

Benedict was a little . . .

uncomfortable.

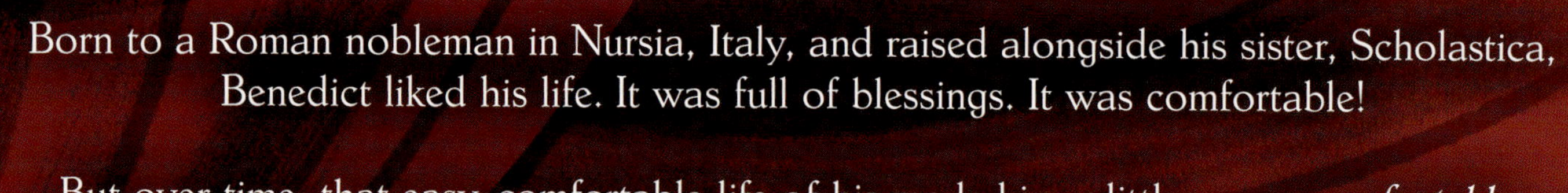

Born to a Roman nobleman in Nursia, Italy, and raised alongside his sister, Scholastica, Benedict liked his life. It was full of blessings. It was comfortable!

But over time, that easy, comfortable life of his made him a little . . . *uncomfortable*.

Benedict knew it deep in his heart: He wasn't made for comfort. Nor was he made for prestige, nor pleasure, nor the other things his peers were seeking. He was made to do the work of God.

So, he said goodbye to his life of comfort—his wealth, his education, his nobility—and, taking his housekeeper Cirilla with him, he left Rome in search of a new life.

A life of work, prayer, study, discipline, sacrifice, and meaning.

A life spent doing the work of God.

He began his new life walking

. . . and searching

. . . and walking.

"Here," Benedict announced to Cirilla, gazing at the remote village ahead of them. "Let's settle here for now."

But after a short time, Benedict's heart longed for even greater solitude, so he secretly fled from the care of the doting Cirilla and found his way to a humble cave in Subiaco.

One, two, three years passed. And in that time, something unexpected happened. This solitary life of fasting and praying became a little . . .

comfortable.

One crisp morning, the faint ringing of a bell pulled Benedict to the mouth of his cave. Peeking outside, he was greeted by a clear sky and chirping birds nesting in the nearby willow.

He smoothed his habit, a generous gift he had received from a monk named Romanus. It was Romanus who, on certain days, discretely delivered Benedict a loaf of bread to this remote spot, hung on a long cord that was fastened with a little bell. And so, Benedict knew it was time for his meager meal.

Now, Romanus was not Benedict's only visitor. There came a small group of shepherds, mistaking him at first for a madman, but finding instead a holy preacher who enraptured them with his teaching. Then, word spread quickly.

Men from the hills

. . . and the villages

. . . and the coastlines,

all carrying heavy hearts, flocked to hear his words of peace.

Suddenly, his secret and secluded home was not so secret and secluded anymore.

Some nearby monks had been persistent in their requests to make Benedict their abbot. He had refused many times, for he had come to like his comfortable life in the cave. But Benedict knew that he was not made for comfort, but for the work of God.

"I will be your abbot," Benedict consented to the monks who approached that afternoon. "But I must remind you again, my rule of life will not agree with yours."

"You are the man God has sent to help us," one of the monks replied. "We are sure of it!"

Benedict followed the monks to their monastery. On the way, he shared with them his thoughts about how they were to live, to work, and to pray.

"Listen carefully, my sons, to the master's instructions, and attend to them with the ear of your heart. This monastery will be a school for the Lord's service," he told them. *"To follow Christ in obedience, do not harden your hearts, but serve the Lord. This is advice from a father who loves you; welcome it, and faithfully put it into practice."*

"We will!" the monks echoed in unison, feet plodding the dirt road and kicking dust into the warm air as they neared their monastic home.

At the monastery, Benedict prayed.

Benedict worked.

Benedict studied.

But the other monks did not prefer to pray like Benedict, or to work, or to study.

The lazy monks considered Benedict's discipline a plague on their previously comfortable lifestyles, and they plotted to get rid of him. Filling his glass of wine with poison, they placed it in front of their young abbot, who reverently raised his hand over it in blessing. No sooner did he begin the Sign of the Cross than the goblet cracked and broke into pieces, the poisoned wine spilling everywhere.

Benedict rose to his feet. "Almighty God, in His mercy, forgive you," he spoke calmly. "Did I not foretell you that my manner of life and yours would not agree?"

Then he left the monastery and its stunned monks, echoing the words of Saint Paul under his breath as he ventured back toward the desert, "By God's grace, I am what I am."

Benedict's virtues and miracles multiplied in the years that followed.

Another multiplication came in the form of monasteries.

One . . . two . . . twelve . . .

More and more men—young and old—flocked to the man of God, ready and willing to not only hear his preaching of peace and beauty, but to live this unique call of obedience, stability, and conversion of life.

"I hope to set down nothing harsh," Benedict told his monks. *"Nothing burdensome. As we progress in this way of life and in faith, we shall run on the path of God's commandments, our hearts overflowing with the inexpressible delight of love."*

It was now the year AD 529. Benedict gazed down from the mountain called Monte Cassino, so high it seemed to touch heaven, where Benedict now prayed, where he worked, and where he studied.

He and his monks had demolished the pagan temple here, and were building up their monastery in its wake. Walking into his cell, he sat down, opened his *Rule of the Master*—crinkled and worn from reading—and grabbed his pen.

Place your hope in God alone, Benedict blended the words together, slowly and thoughtfully. *If you notice something good in yourself, give credit to God, not to yourself . . .*

"Father Abbot!" The voice of one of his monks broke the silence. Benedict dropped his pen and hastened his steps to reach the band of monks who stood outside, worry stretched across their faces.

The monks stood silent, awaiting their abbot's inquiry, not speaking until questioned.

"Tell me, my sons," Benedict looked at the tattered sheet that rested before his monks. It seemed to hold a young boy inside. "What troubles you?"

The monks relayed the devastating story of the young oblate, Severus, buried under the ruins of a stone wall which had crashed as they were building it. They recovered his body to find him bruised, bones crushed, and dead.

Benedict's eyes filled with sorrow, but he was not surprised, for the attacks of the devil were consistent and intense against them. He commanded the monks to rest the boy's body in his cell.

"Now, pray and work," he told them. With that, the weary, worried monks departed.

Benedict entered his cell solemnly, falling to his knees in front of the boy. "In your goodness, Father, you have counted Severus as your son," Benedict shed a tear as he continued his pleading prayer. "By the merits of your Passion and Death, restore him to life, he who is in my safe keeping and obediently doing my work and Yours."

Outside, the monks felt as though they had never worked or prayed so hard, clearing the rubble and doing their best to begin reconstruction of the wall. What a horrible day this seemed to be, but then again, Father Abbot often reminded them to find God amidst the discomfort. Wiping his brow, one of the monks looked up to see a small figure walking toward them. It couldn't be . . .

Severus!

Ever an obedient young Oblate, the boy picked up one of the well-formed bricks and placed it atop another brick laid by his brother monk, as if nothing had happened. “The man of God has done it again!” the monk thought to himself, praising God for the miracle who now stood innocently by his side, ignorant of his own death.

Benedict rose early.

Benedict prayed, but his work was different today. There was a lightness, a joy in his heart.

Today he got to see Scholastica.

His dear sister had also abandoned a life of worldly comfort, and embraced the freeing work of God. Always admiring her brother's way of life, she became abbess of her own monastic community. They both cherished these brief but intimate meetings.

Benedict and Scholastica spent hours in each other's company, discussing God and heaven. A pinkish-orange sunset filled the sky.

"Remind your sisters, dear Scholastica," Benedict encouraged, "*that their way of acting should be different from the world's way; the love of Christ must come before all else.*"

Benedict placed his hand atop hers, admiring the twinkle of sibling love in her eye, and then stood to depart for home. Scholastica, knowing prophetically that this was her last meeting with her brother and that her death was imminent, insisted he stay. Benedict was equally obstinate that he leave.

Scholastica quieted her pleading and bowed her head. If Benedict wouldn't listen to her, God would, she thought. A moment later, thunder began to rumble and lightning lit up the sky. As Benedict turned his neck to look out the window, rain came pouring from the previously clear, color-soaked sky.

He turned back and smirked at his sister.

"Where were we?" Scholastica smiled as she spoke, motioning for her brother to take his seat again. There they remained in prayer and conversation until their departure the next morning.

Benedict prayed. Benedict worked. Benedict studied.

Benedict held his pen weakly and gazed at an image of the Crucified Christ on his desk.

He remembered fondly the dove which rose in the sky on the night his sister went to heaven, shortly after their last meeting. He reflected on his own life of stability and obedience, and his time spent converting his life, daily, to become more like Christ. He hoped it had pleased God.

Are you hastening toward your heavenly home? Benedict etched carefully, with both struggle and determination. *Then with Christ's help, keep this little rule that we have written for beginners.*

He coughed into his habit and took a staggering breath, eager to continue writing.

After that, you can set out for loftier summits . . . and under God's protection you will reach them. Amen.

Regula

"Finished," Benedict sighed. "My little rule for beginners . . . I hope my monks will find it useful."

Biographical Note

Saint Benedict of Nursia died on March 21st, traditionally thought to be in the year AD 547. He predicted his own death, requesting his monks open his tomb six days prior. On the day he was to die, Benedict urged his monks to bring him to the chapel, amidst his severe sickness, so he could receive the Holy Eucharist. He is said to have died standing, raising his hands to heaven in prayer.

It turns out that Benedict's monks did find his "little rule for beginners" useful. Saint Benedict's *Rule of Monasteries*, also known as *The Rule of Saint Benedict*, is one of the greatest classics of Christian spirituality of all time. It has been copied and translated innumerable times, and is adhered to by monasteries and convents all around the world. The *Rule* is remarkably relevant, and even 1500 years after its first autograph, it lives on, reminding Christians that we need deep prayer and a disciplined spiritual life so that we can face the turbulent times we live in and bring peace to a sorrow-stricken world.

Saint Benedict and his *Rule* left a remarkable legacy, laying a foundation for the preservation of Western civilization during a historical period of immense confusion and upheaval. Even in our present day, the influence of his life and the impact of his *Rule* reach beyond monasteries and into all corners of the world.

Author's Note

There have been other books which have beautifully treated the life of Saint Benedict, including his many miracles, only few of which are mentioned in this text. With this project, I wanted to weave his *Rule* into the context of his life, because the two were indeed inextricably connected.

Benedict, of course, lived and breathed faithfulness to the *Rule*, and it was exciting to imagine how the tenets of his *Rule*, impacted by both his Roman upbringing and his faith, as well as the text of other rules, would have appeared in his own speech and writing during the course of his earthly life. Many of the quotes spoken or written by Benedict in *Benedict & the Rule* come directly from *The Rule of Saint Benedict* itself (you will see these excerpts in italics in the story). Other words of his in the story come directly from Saint Gregory the Great's biography on the life of Saint Benedict (the primary source text about his life and miracles). I highly recommend learning more about him by reading this biography, as well as his *Rule*!

Saint Benedict's *Rule* is not only useful for those in religious life. Its foundational principles are meant to inspire our own spiritual lives, and should encourage us in the pursuit of our own rule of life, a powerful way to personalize and concretize our spiritual progress.

In his *Rule*, Benedict teaches the basic monastic virtues of humility, silence, and obedience as well as directives for daily living. The prologue and seventy-three chapters outline how his monks are to work and pray, and it illuminates their vows of stability (commitment to their monastic community), conversion of life (seeking ever-deeper union with Christ), and obedience (which comes from the Latin word "listen," listening first and foremost to the Word of God, and then to one's superior). The *Rule* encourages commitment to prayer, work, study, and hospitality.

These pillars can make up our own rule of life! The aim of a rule is to make and follow practical commitments that help us individually, or as a family, to love God and neighbor and to grow in holiness. When we form good, disciplined habits of prayer and fulfill the duties that God is calling us to in our state in life, the road to sanctity, to total union with Christ, becomes much clearer!

A rule helps us to carry out our true mission. Like Benedict, we were not made for comfort, but for the work of God.

Your rule will be unique and might change over time, but here are some questions and ideas to get you started:

When will you wake up? (Having a consistent wakeup time and bedtime is actually a big help to your spiritual life!)

What will you pray during the day? (Morning offering, the Holy Rosary, the Angelus, etc.) When will you pray and for how long?

What work will you do according to your state in life (as a student, child, parent, spouse, teacher, etc.)?

When and for how long will you read the Bible and meditate on God's Word?

When and for how long will you do your other spiritual reading?

What other devotions will you have or special feasts will you commemorate?

What virtue(s) do you need to work on most?
What vice(s) do you need to rid yourself of most?

How often will you go to Mass or Eucharistic Adoration (outside of your commanded Sunday obligation to attend Mass)?

When will you do your examination of conscience and go to bed?

Visit **FirstFaithTreasury.com/Rule** for a printable template that you can use to create your rule. I strongly recommend customizing and reviewing it with a wise and holy priest or spiritual director!

More from Katie Warner and TAN Books

My True Love Gave to Me: A Children's Catechism for the Twelve Days of Christmas
illustrated by Elizabeth Zelasko

Enchanting artwork meets one of the most popular Christmas tunes of all time. *My True Love Gave to Me* teaches children and adults alike about God's lavishing love for us, and the gifts He bestows on us through His Church. Through memorable rhyme and captivating artwork, numeric symbols help uncover foundational aspects of the Catholic Faith, from the theological virtues to the beatitudes to the twelve doctrines of the Church.

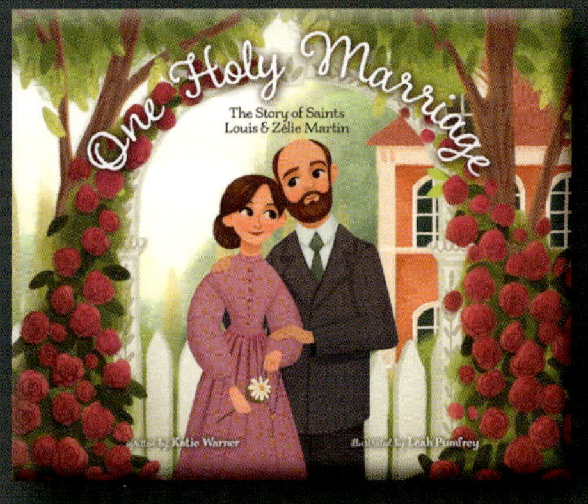

One Holy Marriage: The Story of Louis and Zélie Martin
illustrated by Leah Pumfrey Ballard

Uncover the beauty of the Sacrament of Marriage through the quiet, virtuous lives of Saints Louis and Zélie Martin, the first married saints to be canonized together. This beautiful picture book biography captures the hearts of both child and adult readers, introducing them to the inspirational parents of the Little Flower, Saint Thérèse of Lisieux.

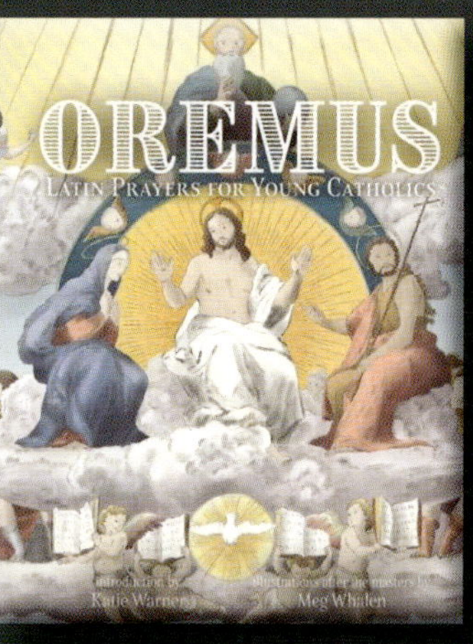

Oremus: Latin Prayers for Young Catholics
illustrated by Meg Whalen

In *Oremus* (Latin for "let us pray") prayers from the Mass and other beloved Catholic prayers, in both English and Latin, are accompanied by master copies of some of the Church's most beautiful artwork. Young Catholics will learn to pray in the language which Pope Saint John Paul II said elicits "a profound sense of the Eucharistic Mystery" while exploring, reflecting on, and being inspired by studies of masterpieces of Christian art, from Fra Angelico to Bouguereau.

Visit FirstFaithTreasury.com to discover more great Catholic children's books.

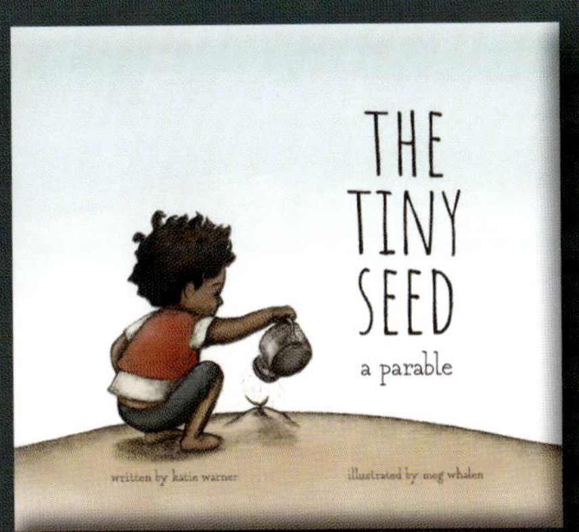

The Tiny Seed: A Parable
illustrated by Meg Whalen

Katie Warner and Meg Whalen bring to life for young readers Christ's famous parable of the mustard seed. Through charming illustrations and a beautiful, scriptural storyline, *The Tiny Seed* reveals the deep truth of our God-given uniqueness, and the incredible process your children will undergo as they grow into the person God wants them to be.

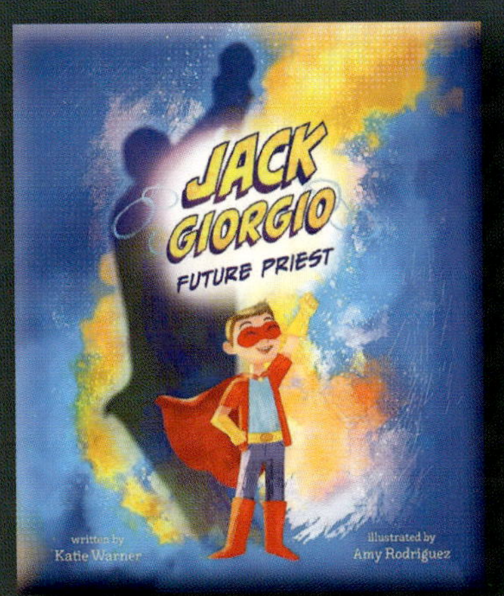

Jack Giorgio: Future Priest
illustrated by Amy Rodriguez

With bright and moving illustrations and a fun, rhyming story, your child will love the spirited Jack Giorgio and his quest to find heroes . . . and become one himself. This beautiful tale shares a touching father-son relationship and emphasizes the heroic nature of the Catholic priesthood, as well as introduces young readers to a host of holy saints and inspires a love for the Blessed Eucharist.

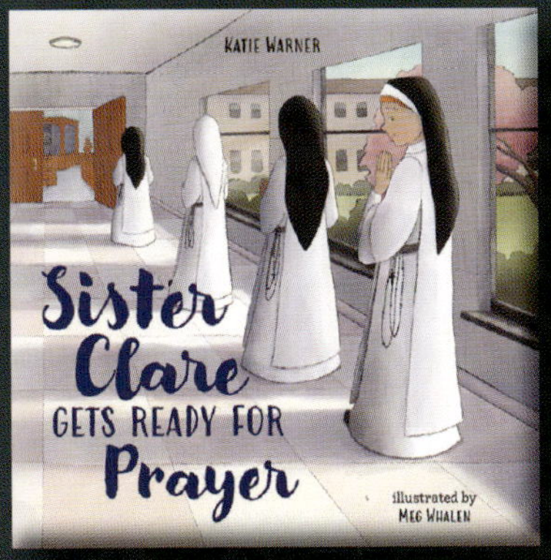

Sister Clare Gets Ready for Prayer
illustrated by Meg Whalen

Sister Clare needs your help getting ready for prayer! Open the cover of this book and you and your child will explore a cloistered monastery together and a day in the life of a Dominican nun. Dance your fingers across the pages, sing, count, move around, and pray; we dare you not to smile. *Sister Clare Gets Ready for Prayer* is the most creative way to introduce your little one to the joy of vocation and the gift of religious life!